BETWEEN TWO WORLDS

BETWEEN TWO WORLDS

Katharine L. Royal

iUniverse, Inc.

New York Lincoln Shanghai

BETWEEN TWO WORLDS

iUniverse books may be ordered through booksellers or by contacting:

iUniverse
2021 Pine Lake Road, Suite 100
Lincoln, NE 68512
www.iuniverse.com
1-800-Authors (1-800-288-4677)

Because of the dynamic nature of the Internet, any Web addresses or links contained in this book may have changed since publication and may no longer be valid.

The views expressed in this work are solely those of the author and do not necessarily reflect the views of the publisher, and the publisher hereby disclaims any responsibility for them.

ISBN: 978-0-595-45939-1 (pbk)
ISBN: 978-0-595-90239-2 (ebk)

Printed in the United States of America

Acknowledgements

In today's society, and specifically living in the midst of the Bible belt, it is hard enough living life as a bisexual with nobody else knowing. Being out is not only difficult, but at times dangerous. Add to that a strong burden to write about my experiences as a part of the bisexual community and the task at hand becomes insurmountable.

Between Two Worlds was a long time coming. I hope that, through this novel two things will happen. First, I hope that other people, whether they are bisexual, lesbian, gay, or trans- gendered, will be able to find the strength to be honest with themselves and others about who they truly are. Secondly, I pray that members of the heterosexual community, specifically Christian members of the religious right, will read this novel and be blessed with a new knowledge and understanding of people like myself. Christians, when following Christianity as Christ intended, can be such a wonderful asset to the GLBT community. They have the power to encourage members of the GLBT community and comfort them and to support them. I pray more encouragement comes of this.

This book would not have been possible without three people. First, my wonderful husband who has shown me over the years what true, unconditional love really is. Through his willingness to learn over the years and be open to new things and new people, I have found a new sense of hope that one day everyone, regardless of their sexual orientation, will be considered equal. Second, my dear friend Dave Klataske. Growing up with various trials I have faced since my birth, I quickly came to have three words I knew more than any other—"can't." and "will never." In addition to my husband, it has been thanks to Dave that I have come to realize the value of someone saying "I believe in you," a statement which has encouraged the formation of Between Two Worlds. Last but not least, Chris Tyner, a wonderful friend and brother in Christ. Through the grueling stages of indecision about publishing between two worlds, Chris was one of few to strike a perfect supportive and loving balance of understanding my trepidation at publishing such a personal work, while also encouraging me that what God had for me to say needed to be said. Without his encouragement, Between Two Worlds might still be sitting on my computer today, unfinished.

Foreword

"Are you saying you're a lesbian?"

"No, but I'm pretty sure I'm bisexual."

This would have been an awkward enough conversation with just about any-one, but I was having it with my husband of nearly two years while lying in bed at 2am on the morning of March 10,2005. Truth be told, we have many of our most profound discussions while lying in bed at night. This, however, I thought would about take the cake as far as a life changing conversation. I was honestly prepared for a very quick divorce after what I felt like was a horrible revelation that late in a relationship.

"Oh, yeah, I kinda figured."

One thing I've learned in marriage is that your spouse will never cease to sur-prise you. Here I thought I was going to be the one busting out the surprise and it ended up being him. He knew?! How?! I'd never told him about past girl-friends, or even crushes. Had he caught me looking at a woman? Damn, I really needed to be more careful about that. I thought I had been. Oh well, he didn't seem mad.

I wish I could say that coming out as bisexual had been the hardest thing I'd ever had to deal with in my life. However, just over 23 years earlier, on Super Bowl Sunday 1982 I had popped into the world greeted by the words "she has a cyst on her back." The next ten years were a blitz of surgery, doctors appoint-ments, pokes and prods, all because of two words; Spina Bifida. To put it in lay-man's terms, sometime while I was being formed in my mother's stomach, my spinal column failed to form all the way around my spinal cord, leaving a hole where a lot of spinal fluid leaked out, along with the nerves that should have gone to the areas below my waist, and formed the aforementioned cyst on my back. I was essentially paralyzed from the waist down, told I'd never be able to have kids, would likely never get married, and might not have the mental acuity to attend college.

Pretty bleak picture to paint for anyone, right? But especially for a young child. I was even told by one unthinking resident at the young age of seven, that if I didn't pay close attention to headaches I might have, I could be dead in a matter of hours from a shunt malfunction. Seemed like everyone thought I was doomed for life as an unproductive member of society; what most would call a "vegetable."

On that fateful night in 2005 I'd already done a pretty good job of beating the odds; I'd gotten married to the man of my dreams a year and a half earlier, gotten pregnant on my wedding night (though we lost the baby a few months later), and although I didn't know it at that time, would graduate college a year later. So I'd spent nearly a quarter of a century dealing with a life changing disability. Wasn't that enough? Wasn't I a minority already? Did I really HAVE to be a sexual minority on top of it?

Well, at least the worst was over. I had told my husband; that would be the hardest part, right? And he was fine with it. Our marriage was fine, nothing was any different than it had been, and from that point on I could go on living life as I had been.

Except not.

1

If I really want to be brutally honest with myself, I can admit that I've known I was bisexual since I was seven years old. I started realizing it around the same time I learned of a family member who is gay. I begged information out of the rest of my family; how did he deal with it? How did he tell the family? How did the family react? What I was told still left me with a lot of questions, but I knew one thing for sure. The strange feelings I'd been having for a few girls I knew at that point were not a good idea to discuss with my family.

So, from that point, I made a decision. I hid. I told nobody about the feelings I had, even when I had a feeling that certain people I was attracted to reciprocated my feelings. There definitely were awkward moments. I was very uncomfortable at sleepovers as a result of this from a very early age. This became problematic because, as a child, I actually had and attended quite a few sleepovers. I rarely ever slept. My parents always thought it was because we stayed up all night talking. We didn't. I was the only one who didn't sleep. While my friends would be snoring away, I would be lying awake, staring at the ceiling, focusing all of my energy on my body and not letting it slip into a semi-conscious state in which I might lose control over it.

Still, I didn't act on anything. At the pre-adolescent stage where most of my female friends were getting all googly eyed at the resident hot boy in the class, I was comfortable around the boys, and very awkward around the girls. Granted I did have crushes on several of the boys as well, but I was able to communicate with them so well, it was never really an issue. After all, it was expected that I'd like the boys. It was the girls I had to be careful around. It was hard enough being disabled and short. I really didn't need another scarlet letter.

Things became unbearable by sixth grade. Normally a very physically affectionate person, I very nearly had a panic attack when certain female friends hugged me, for fear of how my body would respond. I focused most of my energy on keeping myself in check around many of the girls I hung around with and, as a result, never really enjoyed many of the "girly" activities in which I participated. I survived girl scouts for all of a month, if I remember correctly, before feeling like I would lose my mind.

The one thing that might have given me away, or at least caused suspicion, was that I never participated in any of the "gay" jokes that many kids my age were telling. I found them offensive, and didn't think it was any more right to joke about that then it was to make fun of people for their weight, accent, or disability. I'd been told many times by my peers to "loosen up" and "stop being so anal." Contextually, I now find the second comment quite funny. But one thing was for certain; I was different. I relegated myself to the "boys side" of the playground most times, not because I was boy crazy, as many people thought, but because that was where I felt I could be myself. I would later find out that a common aspect of bisexuality is being more physically attracted to one sex and more emotionally attracted to the other sex so, while the physical attraction was still there with some of the guys, it was not as pronounced as the emotional connection which enabled me to better relate to them. The girls, however, I had virtually no emotional connection with. And when things are purely physical; purely carnal, one must be careful.

I survived elementary school with no major mishaps. At that point, I didn't know the word bisexual. I knew what I was, but didn't know there was a word for it except "freak" as I'd come to be called a short time later. All I knew was that I got a "funny in a good way" feeling around certain members of both genders. It wouldn't have a name until many years later.

I went with most of my friends from elementary school to the local junior high school, and that was where my sexuality really became hard to hide. My first year of junior high I realized that we were all at the stage of beginning to figure ourselves out sexually. Unfortunately, that was the year where people started labeling one another. Many of my classmates were victims of stereotyping and were labeled "fags," based on their appearance, voice, or behavior. I would later find out that many of those who were labeled actually are in the GLBT (gay, lesbian, bisexual, trans-gendered) community, but not nearly as many as were labeled by the rest of our classmates.

So seventh grade began with labeling, segregation, and basic chaos. That was the year I met the first person I'd ever known who was like me; an eighth grade girl who liked both boys and girls. I wasn't alone. I was in heaven but, to complicate things further, I was also in love.

Her name was Alex, and she was gorgeous. She was Japanese; stood at a height of five foot three inches, and had slate black hair that fell halfway down her back. I had never seen such shiny hair in all my life. It was like looking at black marble. She used Pantene Pro-V. I never asked, but I knew that smell. She had eyes that were almond in color and in shape, and lips that perpetually seemed to be giving me a flirty pout. With her accent, it always sounded like she was calling me "Katrin" instead of Katharine. Some found it annoying, but I found it endearing.

Smitten didn't begin to describe the state I was in. I had it bad for this girl. It seemed to good to be true. Not only was the physical chemistry there, but we connected on an emotional level as well, which I'd not been able to do with very many females to that point. I wanted to tell the world about her, but I told nobody. I never invited her to come to my house, nor did she invite me to hers. We both had enough trouble keeping things under wraps at school. The last thing either of us needed was our families finding out what was going on.

At the time, I was also crushing on an eighth grade guy; the bad boy type that reminded me of Danny Zuko from Grease. But his name wasn't Danny, it was Rick. He was tall.... six foot already in eighth grade, and really slender. Most would have called him an All-American guy. He had olive skin, was presumably Italian by his looks, and had dark brown eyes and an impish smile. In hindsight, he treated me more like a little sister than a girlfriend, but made no bones about the fact that he was crushing on me. He called me "shorty" and was always very protective of me when we were together. Between the leather jacket, shades, and rebel without a cause attitude, I was ecstatic to have him in my life.

Unfortunately he wasn't a part of my life for long. Not long before the end of my seventh grade year, I was gushing about him to my mom (it surely wasn't safe to gush about Alex, but I had to make sure they knew I was showing some interest in romance..... to make myself look like a normal teenager and all). All too quickly, I learned the meaning of the expression "loose lips sink ships." I'd made some offhand comment about how he was taking a year off before high school because he had to go into rehab for a drug problem. I, personally, didn't view that as much of an issue since most of my friends at the time were into drugs and had no intention of going to rehab. My parents, however, blew their collective gasket. I was forbidden from associating with Rick ever again.

Yet again, hindsight is 20/20. Since they didn't even know who he was or what he looked like, I could have easily continued to hang with him without anyone ever knowing,. However, I didn't. He was getting ready to graduate, and was busy with his classwork, and I busied myself on the other side of campus, hanging with some of the guys from elementary school. I saw him one more time; the day before he graduated. It was just long enough for him to hug me and sign my yearbook. I really hoped I'd see him again. A year and a half later his younger brother told me he had died of a drug overdose that summer.

Rick was no longer a part of my life, but I still had Alex.... for the time being. With summer approaching, toward the end of my seventh grade year and her eighth grade year things became strained between us. We barely spent any time together at all during the week leading up to her graduation. I guess it was just too painful for both of us, as we both realized it was time to say goodbye.

There are definite disadvantages to a seventh grader dating an eighth grader. They only get one year in school together. All too soon, this girl who I had fallen completely head over heels for was gone. I talked to her on the phone a couple of times the summer after she graduated, but I quickly deemed that unsafe as both our parents were within earshot and both of our lives were already complicated enough without our families finding out.

Truthfully I was glad for seventh grade to be over. As I pointed out earlier, that was the year of the name calling. I was four foot six, on crutches and bisexual. I was a prime candidate for being beaten up. And I was. If I had a nickel for every time I was tripped, shoved in a trashcan, spit on, thrown up against a wall of lockers, or had my crutches taken from me I could probably be paying off my college loans more easily today. Even today, I still have a scar on my left thigh from one of my classmates in math class deciding to test whether or not I really had feeling in my legs by stabbing me repeatedly with the back end of a mechanical pencil. I never really had the highest opinion of the intelligence of seventh grade boys.

Eighth grade was actually quite an improvement in my life. A good reputation was easier to uphold that year, as I started dating a guy who most of my friends at the time had crushes on. His name was Joseph. I was envied, but I didn't care. I didn't care about anything or anyone else but him that year. Of course, I was young and in love, so I thought for sure he was the one I would spend my life with. I had fallen in love with a guy and he was in love with me. I could be normal after all. And I could get married. In your face doctors!

Joseph was a romantic; a quality I would later come to realize that I often was attracted to in guys. His hobbies were poetry, drawing, philosophy, and going down the throats of anyone and everyone who gave me trouble. Classic example: in junior high I was given permission to leave class five minutes before the bell rang so I could get to my next class without being trampled. Since most of my classes were upstairs, I was also allowed to have a "friend" go with me to assist with the climb. Naturally I chose Joseph.

On one particular day, I was waiting outside my classroom for Joseph to appear. He showed up right before the bell, huffing and puffing. On our hurried walk down the stairs to my next class, he explained how his math teacher had decided that day not to let him out of class early. Joseph, in response, had at first tried to reason with his teacher for a few minutes and t hen, when that didn't work, overturned a desk, and flipped the teacher off before storming out of the class and running to meet me. Not sure that could pass as entirely romantic, but at that moment I nearly fell over laughing.

In addition to his protective nature, Joseph was also the most handsome guy I'd ever seen. He had already passed the six foot mark (what was it with me and tall guys?) and he was slender, with chiseled features, dark hair and eyebrows that made him look like he was seriously contemplating just about everything that was going on, but that shot up like jumping beans when he sneezed. He had piercing eyes like crystals, but not cold. They had the power to make you feel like you were the most important person in the world when he was looking at you. Of course, maybe that was just when he looked at me. We were, after all, in love. He also had a personality that was like coming home to a warm, cozy fire in the fireplace after a long hard day.

We spent every weekday together and as much time as we could get away with on the weekends. He was great on roller blades and, since he didn't live too far from my house, he would frequently use them for quick transportation to and from visits. One time in particular, he had just left my house and, as usual, called half an hour later when he got home to let me know he was in safe. At the time he called, though, my parents and I were out in the backyard and didn't hear the phone. Apparently, he worried that something had happened, because he took off all over again for our house and arrived out of breath to make sure I was ok before heading back yet again. Just the type of guy he was … and actually still is. We are still good friends today.

Fate didn't smile on me for long, though. My parents decided the local high school wasn't accessible enough for me, and I was to be attending Flintridge Sacred Heart Academy, an all-girls Catholic prep school for the next four years. My dream boy and I broke up the summer after eighth grade; the day I got back from a family vacation in Hawaii.

If there's one thing you really don't want to do to a 13 year old girl who's struggling with sexual identity, it's stick them in a gender secluded environment for four years. As my attraction to women manifested in a mostly physical sense, it was like sticking a straight guy in school in front of the Baywatch babes, and asking them to be able to concentrate on class work.

Leave it to me. As a lowly freshman I had to develop a crush on a senior. Brilliant. Well, at least that was only my first completely unattainable crush. Her name was Josephine and, by this point in my life, I was beginning to realize I had a thing for tomboys. I guessed that made sense because, in actuality, I was often considered a tomboy myself. But I wasn't a tomboy at all compared to Josephine.

She was short, for being eighteen at least. She stood five foot two inches tall and had a very athletic build. She wasn't slender, but rather very sturdy … big boned. She had high cheekbones, full lips, big dark brown eyes, and black hair that was usually pulled back into a ponytail or bun. Every day she wore one of those unisex colognes that always smells like it's still meant for a man. I think that stuff is meant to drive bisexuals crazy.

Josephine was also really popular. Everyone in every grade knew her by name. At lunch time she was always in a huge group of people. That made sense, though, since she was active in several sports and kept busy with student government activities as well.

I was a bumbling idiot around Josephine and spent most of my time attempting to talk to her and kicking myself for the idiot I presented myself as I when I did. Classic example: second semester we had study hall together. We were sitting at a long table reading when she sneezed. Thinking she might finally notice me, I piped up with "gezundheit!" She barely looked up and mumbled a thanks. Gezundheit? What the heck was that all about? Was I German?! I could have at least said bless you. That would have sounded just slightly more personable and might have gotten her to at least look at me. I never seemed to have this problem with guys. Sheesh! Gezundheit! Whatever!

That night I was desperate. I was nearly 14 years old and, at a time where most of my female friends were worrying about their hair, their makeup, and the boys at the neighboring school, I was focused solely on hiding one of the biggest parts of myself. I'd ended up, quickly after freshman year began, hanging out with a group of friends who were largely misfits. Most of them weren't Christian, only one or two of them were Catholic, and none of them ascribed to the "hair and makeup" mentality. Still, I couldn't go on like I was. I didn't see a way life could possibly get any better. I was only 13. With how long the women in my family lived, I'd have about eighty more years of this to endure and if it was hard enough when I was this young, how much worse would it get? When I got home from school I went into the medicine cabinet and took a fist full of pills. Enough was enough. Life shouldn't have had to be as hard as it was, but now it was all over. I could rest. I was told as a child that when I got to Heaven I wouldn't be disabled. From that, I figured that surely in Heaven I wouldn't have to deal with these feelings either. I couldn't wait. Hello freedom!

I lived through it, obviously, but the only thing that night showed me was that I couldn't do anything right. I couldn't even kill myself correctly. Clearly I was doomed to live the same painful reality I'd spent the last six years going through.

I focused the rest of high school on simply getting through and getting it over with. Retreats and over-nights were the worst, but I made it. I completely stayed away from all relationships during high school. It was easier that way. I was tired of the taunts, and increasingly sick of hearing the word "fag."

The end of my junior year things started to really look up … for about two weeks. My friends had convinced me to go to the junior/senior prom and, for reasons I still don't understand, I got the courage to ask the cutest and nicest guy in my youth group at church to go with me. Why I suddenly had to decide I had the courage to ask him out near the end of high school when I'd thought he was really sweet and really good looking since early elementary school was beyond me, but clearly my luck was changing because he said yes. We went, and had a great time. Most of my friends were drooling over my date, which was cool. I was just happy to have him with me. I felt like the luckiest girl in the world.

Junior year ended, and my senior year began. I was rather impressed with myself for making it that far without my sexuality getting me into any real trouble. I had one of my favorite teachers that year, and even decided to attend senior prom. I tried to ask the same guy, but he was going out of town. I went with someone else, and didn't have as much fun as the year before, but it was still worth it.

High school graduation came fast. Almost my entire family was in attendance. Since several of my on again off again crushes were graduating with me and would be hanging out with me most of the day, I wasn't sure how I felt about the whole family being there, but I decided to try to act as normal as possible.

One more summer at home to get through, and then I was out of the house, and away at college. Things just had to get better then. At least I'd be far enough away from my family that t hey really wouldn't know too much about what was going on with me on a day to day basis. And maybe, just maybe, there would be more people like me.

Four months later, with my head held high and my heart filled with hope I left home and headed for my first year of college life. Finally I could really be me.

2

My pillow was so worn from being tossed and turned on there was almost stuffing coming out. My blankets were tied up in knots around my ankles. I didn't sleep a wink the night before leaving for college. I was too excited. I was seventeen years old, and had spent the last ten years battling the nameless enemy of my mysterious attractions. I was old enough, at that point, to be able to rationalize that I wasn't gay because I was attracted to the opposite sex too, but that didn't help the confusion any. I figured getting out of the house and going to college would help me to figure myself out. After all, wasn't college a time of self-discovery for many people anyway?

It wasn't until I started my freshman year that I realized I had a lot of misconceptions about the life I had lived; and specifically the religion I had grown up a part of.

I had been brought up as a Christian and was going to be going to a Christian college; Azusa PacificUniversity. I had decided in high school that I wanted to study to be a pastor. This itself was a huge thing for me since, during most of high school, I didn't really have faith in anything. I guess for me it was just further proof that God calls us when He's ready, not when we are. So this was a huge part of the reason I was so jazzed about going to college. It was a specifically Christian college and many of the students there wanted to be pastors. I figured things would be better in a school where so many people were studying to go into the ministry. This wasn't just a college prep school like the one I had attended and so many of my friends had no choice in attending. This was a school people chose to go to. And Christianity is all about love, right? So I'd be all set. I'd be accepted, I could be myself, and life would get better. Then why did I have that knotted, trembling feeling in the pit of my stomach?

I first heard the word bisexual shortly after moving into my dorm freshman year. I was talking to a friend of mine from junior high and she was telling me that one of the guys I had hung with in eighth grade had come out as bisexual in high school. I felt rather stupid that I'd never really heard the word. Since I was out of my parents' house and there was nobody to see what I was doing, I looked the word up on the Internet. I found a lot of different definitions for the word; including "possessing reproductive organs of both genders." I didn't think that was what she had meant when she had said our mutual friend had come out as bisexual. I knew at that point that the phrase "come out" was most often used in relation to being gay; something that one might not know from an early age. Surely if he had male and female reproductive organs, he'd have known from very early on. I kept looking and found the definition "sexually attracted to both sexes." That was, up to that point, the most freeing experience I'd had. This thing that had been consuming my life for so long had a name: bisexual. That was what I was. All at once it was like one hundred pounds of bricks were unloaded off my back. I could stand upright again, and look the world in the face.

I had made a good number of friends on campus at that point, and as I raced off for morning chapel the next day I planned to talk to a couple of them about my discovery. Maybe I could find more people like me, and maybe my friends could help me understand why I was this way.

That morning's chapel changed everything. Just as the day I'd found out that the smartest thing to do was hide this portion of myself from my family, it was now clear that I had to hide it from everyone at my college campus. The chapel speaker was a man from Focus on the Family. He spent a good portion of his time talking about "same sex attraction." He explained to the school how he used to be attracted to members of the same sex but how, after rigorous counseling, shock therapy, and intervention, he was no longer an "abomination before the Lord." He told everyone that if they knew someone who was struggling with same sex attraction, they too could be healed from the "vice of sin."

At this point I was not only devastated, but very confused. Sin? I'd grown up in a Christian church. I was even a leader in the youth group in high school. I understood sin. Pornography was sin, lust was sin, sex outside of a committed relationship was sin. But being attracted to somebody? I wasn't looking at pornography, I wasn't consumed with undressing people in my mind, and at that point I was still a virgin. So how was I sinning? So much for the brick load on my back being gone; now in its place was a perfectly well defined scarlet letter.

Over the next few months, I decided to delve further into the Christian belief system. I had thought I was ready to begin studying to be a pastor, but if I wasn't aware of this one huge factor of Christianity I wasn't so sure. I simply had to know what was so evil and sinful about me and why. What I found really surprised me. As I sat one morning at 3am in my dorm room in front of my computer, steaming mug of coffee gripped in my trembling hands, I did a web search about same sex attraction and Christianity. At least ten thousand hits appeared on my screen. My head was spinning. How would I ever get through everything before my roommate woke up? I began to click on each link in the order it appeared. I read and read and grew more and more discouraged. The first link I clicked on was a list of verses from the Bible on the topic of homosexuality. As I read, this is what I found:

> Leviticus 18:22 Do not lie with a man as one lies with a woman; that is detestable.

> Leviticus 20:13 If a man lies with a man as one lies with a woman, both of them have done what is detestable. They must be put to death; their blood will be on their own heads.

> 1 Corinthians 6:9 Do you not know that the wicked will not inherit the kingdom of God? Do not be deceived: Neither the sexually immoral nor idolaters nor adulterers nor male prostitutes nor homosexual offenders nor thieves nor the greedy nor drunkards nor slanderers nor swindlers will inherit the kingdom of God.

> 1 Timothy 1:9 We also know that law is made not for the righteous but for lawbreakers and rebels, the ungodly and sinful, the unholy and irreligious; for those who kill their fathers or mothers, for murderers, 10for adulterers and perverts, for slave traders and liars and perjurers ...

> Romans 1:26-27 Because of this, God gave them over to shameful lusts. Even their women exchanged natural relations for unnatural ones. In the same way the men also abandoned natural relations with women and were inflamed with lust for one another. Men committed indecent acts with other men, and received in themselves the due penalty for their perversion.

Now I'll confess that at that moment in my life I found myself guilty of what many Christians in my opinion are guilty of. I stopped. I read these passages, and stopped. There it was, in black and white (or, rather, black and red). Everything in the Bible that related to homosexual behavior was labeled sin and, since bisexuality included the same sex as well as the opposite sex it was, by default, sin as well. I decided that day that, while I would continue my pursuit of becoming a pastor, I would start looking into what the speaker in chapel had been talking about; ex-gay therapy. After all, I believed in God, had always tried to follow Him, and certainly did not want to be "detestable."

In hindsight, I can say thank God I never got as far as the shock treatment that many endure in order to try to rid themselves of same sex attraction. I did, however, spend my first year in college educating myself on the ex-gay movement, and on how I might be able to get rid of my bisexuality. I felt cheated, in a way, that I hadn't been able to put a name to it earlier so that I could have gotten rid of it and enjoyed my high school years. At least now, though, I could be rid of it and enjoy the rest of my life without worrying about it.

I met with a lot of people on campus who said they had experienced years of same sex attraction before being "delivered." I grew frustrated that the first thing they said I needed to do to be rid of it was to pray for God to take it away. I'd been praying for that since I was seven and it still hadn't happened. Next they said I had to remove myself from situations in which I might be tempted. I nearly laughed at that one. How was I supposed to do that? We were at a co-ed school and the running joke at the school was that there were three girls for every guy. In order to do that, I'd have to basically hide in my dorm 24 hours a day. I should have been thanking God that I wasn't attracted to my roommate.

I ended up cutting a few classes halfway through my freshman year because of exceptionally hard days when I knew I'd be tempted. It was awful. I'd never skipped a class a day in my life until that point unless I was sick. But it seemed to be working—I didn't feel nearly as out of control as I'd felt in the months and years leading up to that time, but my grades sure were suffering. Missing classes was taking its toll, and I was amazingly distracted when I was in class.

Halfway through my second year of college, all my efforts went down the drain. I met a girl; well, young woman really. I guess by that point we were past the kid stage; at least most of us. If things were spinning out of control before they had just flown off the handle. Her name was Ann. She was Hispanic; five feet tall, with big brown eyes, a huge smile, thick full lips and silky brown hair that couldn't decide whether it was wavy or curly. I always told her she was shapely and rolled my eyes at her response of "yeah, I guess round is a shape."

This girl was something else. She was definitely my type, she was bisexual, and she was totally into me. At that point I was just about ready to say to hell with the ex-gay therapy. Why did it matter who I was in a relationship with? After all, God is love, and God ordains love, so why should God have a problem with love? If I'd thought the God I loved and worshiped condemned love I don't think I'd have ever worshiped Him to begin with.

The next month was bliss. I saw Ann every day, and sometimes multiple times a day. My roommate started to get a little annoyed that she even stayed over in our room a few nights. For all intents and purposes we were dating. We just knew better than to call it that with the people we were surrounded by. There was talk of people being kicked out of the school if they were found to be engaging in "same sex behavior." Her parents didn't know either, and we both knew we'd better keep it that way.

I wasn't lucky in love for long. She quickly grew unsatisfied with the status of our relationship. She wanted to "take things further." I was content with the way things were. She and I were closer than close, I was also seeing a wonderful guy at the time, and life was just as I wanted it to be. Strangely enough, it didn't actually dawn on me until years later that Craig, the guy I was seeing at the time, didn't know about me seeing anyone else. I had never realized before that I had ever been like that in my relationships. It was rather disheartening. Craig and I are still very close today, but our relationship was always odd. I was very much in love with him, but the physical nature that most romantic relationships take on never progressed past that of friendship. Strangely, I have no regrets. I was truly convinced that Craig and I would end up getting married. I dreamed about it. I felt so safe with him, and he was so charming. Everything from his big dark eyes and impish grin to his goofy Roberto Benigni impersonations and quirky sense of humor endeared me.

I may have been happy that year, but Ann wouldn't be appeased. One day, while I was lounging on my bed watching her work on the computer, she decided she'd had enough waiting. My guard was down, and I didn't expect anything, but the next thing I knew she had stood up, walked to the bedside, and laid down on top of me. I was horrified, asked her what had gotten i nto her, and struggled to get free. She had the upper hand. She was heavier than me and able bodied. She pinned my elbows and knees into the bed. I couldn't even scream. I had heard about this sort of thing happening in heterosexual relationships, but surely not between two women. I couldn't believe what was happening to me, but I suppose that part of me thought that if I just let it happen it would be over fast. After all, a woman couldn't cause too much damage to another woman, right? Wrong. Six weeks later I was diagnosed with Hepatitis B.

My best friend at the time, James, was out of the country during all of this, and he wasn't due to get back for at least another week. That same feeling I'd had in high school began to creep up and I decided I couldn't keep going. I was disabled, bisexual, and had been raped. How much of an outcast, how far from the norm could one person be? I was still at least half way convinced that God loved me at that point. Surely if I was able to just end it before anyone was able to do anything else to me, I'd be in Heaven. I'd be safe. That was the only safe place. I was sure of that now.

I had decided what to do. I wasn't as wet behind the ears as when I had tried to take my life a few years earlier. I knew what would kill me and what would just severely incapacitate me. I had researched enough to know that I had to do things just right, otherwise I'd wake up three weeks later in a hospital and would essentially be a physical and mental vegetable for the remainder of my life. So this time I planned. I had an assortment of pills in my dorm room in a storage bin under the bed. I now knew what I needed to do. I knew how many to take and how and when do it so that I wouldn't risk anyone finding me before the drugs had time to do their job. I would do it that night after dinner when my roommate went to her evening class.

That night I went to the cafeteria for dinner with my roommate as always. As we finished our meal, I looked around the room, thinking that would be the last time I saw it or any of the people in it. We walked to the front of the cafeteria and as we walked out the front door, neither one of us could believe who we saw. James, who was supposed to be in Egypt for at least another week, had come back early. If I was losing faith in God at that point, it came back that night. I really felt he'd been sent back early for a reason. James and I talked that night about everything that had happened, and I felt relieved. Still, though, even with how much I trusted him I couldn't bring myself to tell him about my bisexuality. I simply didn't know if it was safe.

In the months that followed, the hepatitis went out of control. I had done my homework on the form that I had, and had high hopes initially. Apparently, symptoms don't manifest for everyone who contracts it. For some it just lies dormant. I had hoped I'd be one of the lucky ones. Didn't seem like that was in the cards, though, based on what was happening.. My weight was fluctuating up to ten pounds a week, I was weak and shaky and I looked like a ghost. I really wasn't happy about the weight thing, as I'd just ended a two year struggle with bulimia. Oh yes, my other skeleton in the closet.

Around the middle of junior high school my family started giving me a hard time about my weight. I was really upset. Up until I was about twelve I'd always had my family bragging about my "hourglass figure." I wasn't the least bit self conscious about my body, minus my disability. That was the only thing I really felt like I had. That all seemed to change when puberty hit. Suddenly everything I ate, drank or looked at caused me to gain wait. I couldn't keep it off and the more I felt like I was being judged by my family because of it, the more I was told that if I kept getting fatter I'd end up confined to a wheelchair, the more desperate I got. I would binge and purge so much in a day that there was hardly a time gap between what went in and what went out. I'd seldom eat with others around me and when I didn't purge I'd intentionally eat things that I knew would upset my stomach, thus making me lose more weight. It actually got so bad that the summer before my sophomore year of college I started taking ephedra pills and worried greatly one night that I was having a heart attack. It was very out of control.

It was James, actually, who helped me to stop. He was the one who told me that I needed to realize the most important thing wasn't how others saw me. They couldn't decide my life for me. I had to remove myself from the controlling grip that others had on my life.

So I was able to little by little stop my unhealthy eating habits. Not two months later, I was slammed with the hepatitis. Again, the weight was up and down, the thin layer of hair on my arms thickened to compensate for the loss of body heat, and I started getting blotchy patches all over my skin. Luckily, it didn't hit as hard as it could have. Things seemed to plateau a few months later, and I started to feel a little better. Life moved on.

Just after I'd been diagnosed with the hepatitis, my relationship with Craig ended. He had been going to Azusa Pacific with me our freshman year. It was at the end of that year that we started dating. Over the summer between my freshman and sophomore year of college, I found out that his funding for the next year had been cut and he would have to go to another school. I was crushed. We continued dating through the summer, right up until a few days before his birthday in November of my sophomore year. Then it ended; suddenly and without warning one night while we were talking over the Internet. I couldn't figure out why. I was now completely alone.

I guess you could say I was relationship hopping in those days because, yet again, I wasn't alone for very long.. Just a couple of weeks after the breakup I was introduced to another guy over the Internet, Don. I should have known that was going to be a disaster from the start. He was in the same class as my roommate's younger sister; still in high school when I was a sophomore in college and two years younger than me. I never in a million years imagined being in a relationship with a younger man.

Somehow, I allowed him to sweep me off my feet. It was the end of November and he was talking with my roommate one night. I'd heard of him before but never thought much of it. He was just my roommate's sister's friend. That particular night, they seemed to be having an amusing conversation. My roommate kept laughing and telling me what Don was saying. At one point I quipped back and told her something to respond to him with. He responded to her to say something to me and, after half an hour of my roommate playing monkey in the middle, she gave him my contact information. We met over the computer that night and talked for three hours. We talked every night for two weeks, for several hours a night. Then, the second week in December, he decided to come out to the campus for a couple of days to visit. I was in no place to be in a relationship at that point. My heart and mind were very confused and it wasn't a good idea, but I didn't seem to recognize that. I was an idealist and a romantic and when, very quickly, this knight in shining armor asked me to marry him I said yes.

The whole thing was really quite unplanned, as the engagement was to be five years long due to military obligations. In actuality, though now I have been married to my husband for three years, if I were still with Don right now we still would not be married. The date for the ceremony was set for December 9, 2006. It was immature, stupid, and idealistic. Still, I loved him and was convinced he was the one I was going to spend the rest of my life with.

We were together for a year and a half. At that point, I just couldn't take it any more. We weren't going anywhere … it was to be a very long time before we would be married, and although I was still convinced that we were going to get married if things kept going the way they were, I was no longer sure that I was happy with that. I felt like I was settling, rather than marrying out of passionate love. Truth be told, I didn't want to be a soldier's wife. It didn't fit me. Worrying about my husband jumping out of planes every day, being separated constantly, raising a family essentially alone and moving every few months just wasn't for me. It was hard because I loved him very much, but with the way things were going, I didn't feel like we were in love, and I definitely didn't feel like what we had was the kind of love that formed a marriage. We broke up just before he was to go to basic training the summer after my junior year of college.… two months before I met the man who I would later marry.

Senior year, honestly, was when things really started to get challenging for me. Barely six weeks after I broke up with Don, my friend Abe called me up and told me that he was going on a road trip the weekend before classes started. He wanted me to go with him. He then dropped the bomb on me. Micah Royal had moved to southern California and was going to be attending the same college as we were.

I had heard about Micah a year earlier. A girl named Stephanie had started attending Azusa Pacific and she was originally from North Carolina. She was a friend of Micah's. She and I struck up a friendship and one day she was telling me about North Carolina and she mentioned Micah. The more she talked about him, the more I thought that the guy couldn't possibly be real. He sounded too good to be true. He was a Christian, studying to be a pastor. He was good looking (I'd seen a picture), apparently family values were very important to him (he comes from a big family) and from everything that Stephanie told me he was amazingly sweet. I remember laughing with her when she told me about him and saying "let me know if this dream guy ever decides to move to California. I'll marry him." That's what I get for being sarcastic.

The weekend before we were to go on the trip, Abe had given Micah my phone number so that we could coordinate who was going to bring what in terms of picnic food. I liked him immediately. He and I talked on the phone and laughed and joked about how silly Abe and his girlfriend were with their googly eyed love stares. We were both just out of serious relationships and found other couples disgusting at best. It sounded like he and I would be able to just go off and have some fun and leave the couple to their own devices.

The day of the trip was great. Micah and Abe picked me up at my apartment and we were off. Micah and I talked the entire way in the car. It was to be a three hour trip; not long at all. However, Abe was distracted and had given Micah the map. Since Micah had only been on t he west coast for a few days, he didn't know where things were. We were supposed to be finding a city named Bakersfield but thanks to his expert navigation skills, we took more than a few wrong turns and, seven hours later, ended up in a city called Baker. Between that and a scare at the gas station where a distracted Abe drove off with the gas pump still in the car, we were having an eventful day.

We ended up spending around eighteen hours together that first day. When we got to Bakersfield, we went off and played video games and skeet ball while the love birds had some alone time. We found out a lot about each other. Micah was a college graduate and was in graduate school where I went to college studying to be a pastor. Right from the start we had that in common. The big difference was that he had a church he was already on track in; the Worldwide Church of God. Before long, I started attending with him and we both did a lot of ministry work together. We spent every day together for six months, but weren't dating. It made me crazy. Something in me apparently had known all along that he was the one I was meant to be with. But he didn't seem interested. That was what I didn't get. I was wildly in love with him and trying hard not to show it. Everyone else seemed to think he felt the same way, but there was no sign of it. We were simply the best of friends. Then, all in the span of three days, we went from just best friends, to dating, to engaged. We got married six months later.

3

"Why would a loving God create someone with an attraction that it was wrong to act on?" Micah and I really started having conversations along these lines early in our marriage. This one was on the way up to Big Bear, CA on our honeymoon. My theology, at that point, had become even more confusing than it had become during college. After doing some more research, I was starting to believe that it wasn't the attraction that was sin, but acting on it. This, of course, brought about the previously mentioned question. And so the cycle started all over again.

I was really blessed to marry someone who has an open mind to issues like these. When I first met him, Micah didn't believe acting on same sex attraction was approved of in the Bible, but he also didn't believe the orientation was condemned. Little did we know we both had a lot to learn in the months and years to come.

By that point, we were ministering side by side in the same church he'd been in since long before we met; two, actually. The head pastor was over both a church in Pasadena and one in Inglewood. The commute was deadly, but it was fun. The people were nice, and we felt very much at home. Women weren't, at that point, allowed to be ordained in the Worldwide Church of God, so I had to be content with ministering without a title. It didn't really matter that much in the big scheme of things. I was still doing what I love with the man I love.

Now looking back on the last few years in our marriage, we often say that we have been through more in three years than most people go through in fifty years. Two months after we got married, I was already knee-deep in what should have been my last year of college. I was very excited at the prospect of finally being done. In my mind, it would be another "in your face" to the doctors who had painted such a bleak picture of what my life would be like. It also felt good because for the past four years I hadn't felt like anyone, except Micah, had actually believed I had what it would take to graduate college. It was nice to finally have someone who I really felt believed in me.

As I was sitting having lunch with my former college roommate one afternoon, I suddenly began to feel very dizzy and weak. I stood up to go and get a drink of water and, as I did, what seemed like an ocean of blood poured from me. The next half an hour or so was a complete blur, but what it came down to was that I had become pregnant on our wedding night and, since I was taking birth control at the time, the baby had been injured so severely that the pregnancy could not continue. I hadn't even known that I was pregnant. I was under the misconception that "the pill" was foolproof. Boy, was I wrong.

The following month was horrendous. Not that there is ever a good time to have a miscarriage, but October of 2003 in Southern California; specifically in Glendora, was a really bad time. It was at that time that horrible fires broke out in the area. Everything around us was ablaze. The hills above us were charred, our campus was covered in ash, and the smoke in the air was so thick it was hard to see. So, just days after we had lost our first child, who my husband named Eve Glory, we decided it would be best to heed evacuation warnings in our area and bunk out at my parents' house for a couple of nights. That was especially difficult for me since I frankly didn't want anybody knowing at that point about what had happened. I was extremely devastated and frankly still very sick. I was not looking forward to it.

The night we arrived at my parents' house, just prior to going to bed, I broke the news to them. My mother didn't really react very much but, later that night, my father walked into the kitchen where I was getting a drink of water and said he understood how much pain I must be going through and how sad he was to hear what had happened. That helped a lot.

The next day I had an appointment to have what is called a D&C. It's a technical term for an operation that women have to have after they have a miscarriage to make sure there isn't any dead tissue that gets left in their body.

The experience was wretched. It would have been bad enough just having the procedure done, but as it turned out I picked the wrong hospital to have it done. As I lay down on the table, I fully expected an IV to be started or at least some drugs to be administered. Instead, the doctor went about with the procedure without so much as a sedative or a painkiller. When I l oudly protested, the response was "you're not supposed to be able to feel anything below the waist, so what does it matter?" It didn't help much that, when I had the post-op ultrasound later t hat day the doctor had a horrified expression on her face and said there was a huge growth on my uterus. They sent me home to a horrendous day of torment worrying that I might have some form of cancer, only to get a call the next day from the doctor saying "you know that growth we were talking about on your uterus? Turns out you're fine.… it's a perfectly healthy ovary." Suddenly I understood all too well what my grandfather meant when he told me "doctors are just practicing medicine."

As a result of the malpractice, I was very ill for nearly a month following that day. I tried to file malpractice against the hospital, only to find out that the hospital had been shut down for repeated reports of such things in the previous months. I had already missed several weeks of classes at that point, and knew that I was going to have to withdraw for the rest of the semester. There was no way I could make it up soon enough, especially with finals right around the corner. Frankly, I was fairly fed up with the school's reaction to what had happened. I even had one professor who told me that I should have let him know ahead of time when I would be missing classes, as if I had planned to have a miscarriage.

After a short battle, I finally convinced the financial aid office not to charge me for the month I'd already been in school. I told them I was going to try to re-enroll the next semester. Little did I know, that was going to be far from possible. Because of the fact that I wasn't in classes, I was no longer eligible to keep my job at the school library. That was the only job I had, and had been really helping our income since I started working there the previous June. At that point, it was just down to Micah's pastoral work at the church. With rent, a car payment, insurance, utilities, and debt making ends meet was nearly impossible. When I went back to the financial aid office in late December to attempt to re-enroll I was told I would have to pay a tremendous amount out of pocket because of being past financial aid dates for that semester. It was hopeless. At that point, I was really starting to believe I wasn't going to graduate college. I had gotten so close!

The summer of our one year anniversary, we got a sudden church transfer. We had been living in Glendora, CA in a very overpriced one bedroom apartment, and ended up moving on very short notice to San Bernardino, CA to work with a circuit of smaller churches. Things were great. We really liked the pastor and his wife with whom we would be working, and our new place was really close to some old friends of mine.

Our lives seemed set before us. There were some openings coming available where Micah might be able to pastor full time, most excitingly to us, a few in North Carolina where he grew up. I'd wanted to leave California since I was a child. I loved adventure. I was ready for something new, and I was thrilled at the idea. We were in a church we both really enjoyed, and we were happy together. What more could we ask for? Little did we know our lives were about to be changed forever, and the direction of our ministry was about to take an about face.

The day we started moving into our apartment in San Bernardino, the first person to great us was a very boisterous woman in a wheelchair. She was the grandmotherly type; with short hair and a big smile. She lived across the courtyard from us. She told us that she and her partner lived together. They were a lesbian couple. She seemed really nice. We talked for a while, she found out that we were in ministry, and she asked us if we had any ministry commitments for that Sunday. We didn't, and so she invited us to go to her church with her. We tentatively agreed. After she left, Micah and I talked about how we felt about what had happened. Neither of us had a problem with her being a lesbian, but we weren't sure how we felt about her living with her partner and, presumably, being sexually active with one another. We decided we'd attend church with them that weekend, though, just to see how it would go.

Sunday came quickly. The church was amazingly friendly. Everyone welcomed us with open arms. Our neighbor joked that we were here "token straight friends" and that their church was so accepting it welcomed straight people too. We all laughed at that. Just before we got to the church that day, we had been introduced to another friend of our neighbor's; a transsexual. Her name was Melissa on the weekends and in our apartment complex but, because she still lived with her parents, it had to be Marshall the rest of the time lest anyone find out. Micah s eemed a bit surprised and ill at ease at first but, since I'd known another transsexual in junior high school, I didn't think much of it. She seemed nice.

Lots happened in the weeks following. We found out that Melissa stayed with our neighbors most of the time. And she ended up spending quite a bit of time at our place, too. She helped us unpack, kept me company when Micah was on errands, and basically just allowed us the privilege of getting to know her.

A few weeks later, we found out that Melissa had been kicked out of her house because her family had heard rumors that she "dressed like a girl." She had no place to go and our neighbors' apartment was too crowded as it was. Micah and I looked at each other and silently nodded before offering to her that she could stay with us for a while until she got herself on her feet. She was shocked, but agreed. A few days later, she had all of her stuff moved in and stored under the futons in our living room.

I guess it would have been too much to ask for things to settle down for a while at that point. Our neighbors and new bunkmate had come with us to a picnic our church was hosting. That seemed to go fairly well. No real problems. However, a week later Melissa decided she wanted to come to church with us. We agreed, and she came with us that weekend. She seemed to really enjoy the church and even liked our pastor, to whom she confided in that she was a transsexual. Things, again, were fine … until the next day.

Micah and I were having our weekly meeting with the head pastor and his wife to assess our progress in the ministry, the week's work, and where to go from there. The only issue that was really discussed was Melissa. The pastor encouraged us to begin ex-gay therapy with her, and said that the church had threatened to split if she came back. He said if she did come back there would have to be a meeting about where she could use a bathroom, who she was and wasn't allowed to be alone with, and what proper protocol for her incorporation into the church would be.

As we had done a lot of research into the subject in the previous weeks, Micah and I tried to explain the ins and outs of being a transsexual; how it wasn't a mental illness, was caused in the mother's womb when the brain developed as one gender due to the hormone bath, and the physical body developed another gender. They looked at us like we'd each grown another head. It was not a pleasant meeting.

We weren't even out of the parking lot that afternoon when we'd reached a decision. Micah would send in his resignation letter to the church office. So began the ministry that God had set forth for us to do from the beginning. We just didn't know it yet.

It was just past our one year anniversary. We didn't have a home church, but we decided to start attending church with our neighbors again. The people were nice, and we liked the openness and acceptance the church offered. We stayed there for about six months. In March of 2005 some issues with the apartment complex we were living in caused us to have to move. We relocated to the nearby city of Colton. It was here that our personal ministry really took off.

Not long after we had settled into our new apartment in Colton we both felt a strong calling to start a church of our own. We'd been in contact with some people who had done the same and had received guidance in matters of the business aspect of it. We felt as though there weren't churches that we had found that had the mission we hoped to achieve. We didn't want a "gay church" which we felt like the one we'd recently attended was, and we didn't want a "straight church" which we'd attended in the past. We wanted a church that brought together people of all types; all orientations, backgrounds, races, etc.

Yes, our theology was evolving. We'd come a long way from our honeymoon conversation a year and a half earlier, and I'd come even farther since my days of pursuing ex- gay therapy. I must pause for a moment here, though as I realize it would not be very fair to say all of this without explaining the research we did and the reasons for the beliefs we adopted and still maintain. Remember the passages I found on the Internet that night in my dorm room? Remember how I said I was making a mistake and stopping at just reading what they looked like they were saying on the surface? Well, eventually Micah and I both developed the courage to look deeper.

> Leviticus 18:22 Do not lie with a man as one lies with a woman; that is detestable.

This seems pretty straightforward, doesn't it? On the surface, it looks as though homosexual sex between two men is being condemned. And it is, in a way. Focus for a moment on the word detestable. In most translations, it says "abomination." The original texts use the term to'eba, which means abomination. However, to'eba doesn't mean sin. Wearing mixed fabric clothing and eating "unclean" meat were also referred to as to'eba. To'eba is a cultural taboo of sorts; something that a culture of people deems unclean, or wrong, or impure. Nothing suggests that these same taboos are actually sinful in the eyes of the Lord.

> Leviticus 20:13 If a man lies with a man as one lies with a woman, both of them have done what is detestable. They must be put to death; their blood will be on their own heads.

Again, a cultural rule. It says nothing of what God's views on this matter are, only what the cultural punishment for this "offense." is.

> 1 Corinthians 6:9 Do you not know that the wicked will not inherit the kingdom of God? Do not be deceived: Neither the sexually immoral nor idolaters nor adulterers nor male prostitutes nor homosexual offenders nor thieves nor the greedy nor drunkards nor slanderers nor swindlers will inherit the kingdom of God.

> 1 Timothy 1:9 We also know that law is made not for the righteous but for lawbreakers and rebels, the ungodly and sinful, the unholy and irreligious; for those who kill their fathers or mothers, for murderers, for adulterers and perverts, for slave traders and liars and perjurers ...

In these two passages, when they are read in their original languages, two terms are used. Malakoi means "soft" or "weak." A lot of people think it means effeminate, but nothing in the original texts support this. Malakoi doesn't mean the same thing as pederasty, which is love, often sexual love, of a man for a young boy. However, malakoi is a term that was used in first century C.E. to describe people involved in this type of behavior. Because of this, the use of the term malakos makes a lot of sense in reference to a call boy.

Arsenokoitai, also used in this passage, is a combination of two words meaning "male" and sexual intercourse," but the nature of this sexual activity is unknown.

As recently as the twelfth century, lists of verses pertaining to homosexuality did not list either 1 Cor 6:6-10 or 1 Tim 1:10. Frankly that wouldn't make a lot of sense if the clear meaning of t he passage referred to homosexuality. These passages may be taken to refer to male sexual activity such as prostitution, or pederasty as I mentioned before, but whether homosexuality is included in this can't be proven. One thing can be determined from these texts, though, and that is the condemnation of exploitive sexual acts such as prostitution and the use of children as sexual objects by adults.

Finally,

> Romans 1:26-27 Because of this, God gave them over to shameful lusts. Even their women exchanged natural relations for unnatural ones. In the same way the men also abandoned natural relations with women and were inflamed with lust for one another. Men committed indecent acts with other men, and received in themselves the due penalty for their perversion.

If you can believe it, I've actually had this one tossed at me more than any of the others. And it's actually the easiest to explain once you get into the historical context. This passage describes the events of a fertility ritual celebrated in honor of pagan gods. The belief of the people engaging in the ritual was that the gods were appeased by sex. The more sex the people had, the happier they believed the gods would be. Therefore, they engaged in as much sex as was possible. It wasn't just men having sex with women, or women having sex with women or men having sex with men. From the way many history books have portrayed it, it was men and women having sex with essentially anything and everything they could in an effort to please the gods.

When you realize that, the passage makes no sense as one that would condemn homosexual relationships any more than heterosexual relationships. The people I know who are in homosexual relationships don't believe it to be just about sex for sex's sake. It's about love. Love is not depicted in the above passage, but rather just the physical act of sex. Once you've looked at the history, it should be easier to see why we came to a point where we could no longer believe a loving God really condemns love between two people, regardless of their gender. Love isn't wrong, but perversions of it like rape and pederasty are. In much the same way,

Christianity is not a religion of intolerance and hatred, but certain perversions of it are. I realize that now. I wish I had earlier.

So now we're back in March of 2005; back during that eventful night when I decided to share the one secret I'd always kept with the man I love. By that point, I'd already come to the conclusion that homosexuality wasn't a sin. I'd concluded that homosexual sexual acts weren't sinful. And I had come out to my husband as having had an attraction to the same sex since a very early age. It didn't really seem as though there was that much left to do. The difficult part was over. Little did I know that that night opened up another chapter of my life; a chapter of questions, soul searching, moral qualms, and the drive to change lives.

4

Growing up, my friends used to ask me if I wished I hadn't been born physically disabled. Duh! They would also ask me a lot what it would be like for me if I woke up one morning and suddenly didn't need my crutches anymore. They were always shocked by my answer. Most everyone seems to think that would be the happiest day of my life; a day filled with nothing but joy. In reality, though, it would be just as scary as if I'd never been disabled a day in my life and suddenly woke up one day without the ability to walk. What most people don't understand is that when you've lived a certain way all your life and then suddenly that changes, it's not just whoops and hollers. It's scary. You feel like everything you once knew is gone. Sure, the change might be for the better, but change is never easy, even when it's good, and change is stressful.

I got a good taste of this when I came out to my husband that night. I went from hiding for 23 years and not showing anyone that part of me to having the one person with whom I was and am the most intimately connected know my secret. To make matters worse, I really didn't know what to make of him saying he pretty much already knew. I mean, on the one hand, that should have been comforting because if he already knew then not much would change. On the other hand, if he already knew, who else knew? What did they know? How much? What did they think? I'd never felt more watched in all my life as I did in the days that followed when I went out in the community. I found myself silently asking "can they tell?" whenever I saw someone walking by. "Do I look bisexual?"

This surely didn't seem very freeing at all. At least before I came out I was in blissful ignorance of the fact that anyone could possibly know I was any different from the "norm" when it came to my sexuality.

As I said before, I thought that Micah would be the hardest person to come out to, because I had it in my head that my sexuality would affect my relationship with him more than with anyone else. That was a logical thought, but I wish my experience had followed it.

During the time in which all of this was going on, I wasn't in contact with my family. From time to time, though, Micah was. During one of his communications with them, he wrote about how proud he was of how I was dealing with coming to grips with my bisexuality. I realized right then that, when I one day was to talk with my family again, it would be very awkward. I couldn't have been more right. I started talking to them about nine months later and things were expectedly awkward. I still don't think most of them really understand what bisexuality is really all about and, specifically, what it means in my case.

I mentioned earlier the trials that I came to be faced with once I came out. While I was still in the closet, so to speak, I didn't have to deal with how I felt about bisexuality, how I thought it should be lived out, and how it would play into what, as far as society is concerned, was a heterosexual marriage. Now, though, I was faced with all those questions.

I was especially troubled by my past in the context of what I'd understood about many bisexuals. I'd been involved with two girls in my past; first in seventh grade, and then my freshman year of college. During both of those relationships, I was also seeing a guy at the time; though during the first the guy and I weren't "official." From all the research I'd done it seemed as though most bisexuals engaged in relationships with both genders at the same time throughout their lives; both emotionally and as sex partners. Talk of threesomes was widespread. Though I had been seeing two people at once back then, I found that I had a problem with the concept of being married to my husband and being with someone else in that way at the same time, whatever their gender. Whereas with my exes I was never sexually active (of my own will at least), now I quite clearly was, and marriage added a whole new dimension to the issue.

Once again, I went back to Scripture. I was even more conflicted at that point, as all throughout the Bible men had multiple wives. I started to wonder if that was a sign that the lifestyle I had come to know as being lived by a "typical bisexual" was acceptable in God's eyes. I never quite came to believe that, though, and just as I was starting to, all the misgivings I had led me back to Genesis and to the creation story specifically. That was where I found my answer. I can't say for sure whether this is right or wrong but what I gained from that was that, in God's original plan there were two people who loved one another and were with one another romantically; Adam and Eve. I was past the part, at that point in my life, where I bought into the mindset that because the first two people God created were a man and a woman, that showed that only heterosexuality was natural. That was an easy mindset to debate with. After all, the first two people would have to have been male and female, otherwise how would the world have populated?

However, the creation story did have something to it that I felt applied to my trials. The original example of romantic love between two people in the Bible involved two people. Only two. In my experience of marriage, it would be nearly impossible, if not completely impossible to give yourself fully to more than one person. There would always be one of them who knew a part of you the other didn't. There would always be competition.

This was the point in my life where I decided to live a life permanently like I had been living since my husband and I started dating. It would be my husband and me, and nobody else. I had gone from being a closeted bisexual, to a bisexual, to a monogamous bisexual. Things started to feel more settled. I had figured myself out.

What was to come from this decision was much more surprising than my straight friends' responses to finding out about my sexuality. After only a short time, I was already used to getting hate mail both from former church members and friends and also from random people who viewed my Internet profile and decided they didn't like me. To this day, every few weeks I still get a "Jesus hates fags" virus on my computer. But I got used to it. It hardly fazes me anymore. Like my mother always used to say, "we all have our cross to bear."

What did and still does faze me is the discrimination I still get from many people who are also in the GLBT community. I get gay people telling me that bisexuals are greedy because they "have to have both." I get trans people telling me I'm just confused, and, worst of all, I get bisexual people telling me I'm not really bisexual if I'm only with one person. I literally exhaust myself explaining to people that bisexuality is an orientation, not an action and that, by their logic, nuns and priests didn't have sexualities because they don't have sex with anyone.

5

In the midst of all of this self-discovery, I was also keeping busy alongside of Micah pastoring our newly created Safe Haven Community Church. Shortly after moving to Colton, we had begun getting to know some people in the area; specifically members of the GLBT community. Though Melissa had been attending church with our neighbors in San Bernardino, she decided to begin coming to Safe Haven in order to help us with our sound system for worship.

Shortly after Safe Haven became a registered church and had everything in place, it was time for one important thing that I had been waiting for since high school. After all those years, I was finally about to be ordained. This time it was for real. Micah organized the ceremony, my favorite teacher from high school preached that day, I was presented with an ordination certificate and Micah performed a worship dance taught to him by one of our other church members to the song "Bless The Broken Road." It was the perfect ordination ceremony.

Though it was a small church, Safe Haven was mighty. We had a core group of about five people, and could have up to twelve on a busy Sunday. We achieved our mission of creating a church that was open to and included all populations. Though the transsexual population of Safe Haven was significantly larger than other populations, we also were able to incorporate the physically and mentally disabled population, a variety of different races, and people of several different religious backgrounds. As a result of that last grouping, we ended up structuring a worship service that met in the middle between that of a Protestant church and a Catholic church. We held communion every week, and had prayer requests voiced for people in our family and in the community. We had worship songs each week, Scripture readings, and always the main sermon.

Perhaps the most moving part of the services was a regular part of our worship team; a 29 year old man named Collin. Collin was born with spastic quad cerebral palsy. He was in an electric wheelchair and had a hard time speaking. He also had a gift for connecting people to God in a way they could understand on a very deep level. This was an especially wonderful gift for Micah and me to witness since, when we met Collin, he wasn't sure he believed in God any longer. He had been raised Mormon and was even engaged to a woman once before. However, he had known for some time of his attraction to men. He also knew that the religion he was brought up a part of condemned same sex behavior and thought homosexuality as a whole was extremely sinful and a perversion of God's plan. Through sharing our testimony with Collin, he was able to once again find God's love. But anyway, I digress. Collin's wonderful way of helping other people connect to God was that he performed worship dances. He would get out of his wheelchair, kneel on the ground, and wave colorful cloths in intricate designs to the rhythm of worship and praise songs. His worship dances were so beautiful and so graceful that they spoke wonders about his relationship with God. People who just met him who would otherwise be somewhat uncomfortable around someone with such a severe disability often remarked that they forgot he was disabled when they watched him do that. I found it very appropriate that the first song I ever saw him do a worship dance to was called "Look At Yourself Through Heaven's Eyes."

Another blessing in our church was a man named Ken. Ken lived in the same group home as Collin and another of our worship members, Grace. Ken was in his forties and classified as severely mentally retarded. He was unable to read, could not converse past simple questions and answers, yet had the most loving presence about him, and a spirit that was willing to help those in need whenever he could. Although it was nearly impossible to converse past a simply how are you what are you doing today, I marveled at the fact that he almost felt like a father figure to me When Safe Haven was meeting at the park nearby, he would help Micah set up the audio equipment and the communion table before church each week. When we held our monthly pet ministry events at the local retirement home, he would take charge of helping pass around several of the animals for the people to hold and play with. When we had lunch as a church, he would help feed Collin, who had trouble eating on his own. That was just the sort of person he was.

One particular day I was feeling a heavy burden on my spirit about Ken. I knew he had a wonderful relationship with God…. it was evident in his praise, and his service to others. He couldn't pray verbally, but always chorused an "amen" after every prayer and lifted his hands high, humming with all his might during worship. Every time I thanked him for helping out at church, his joyful, gravelly voice chirped the response "it's for baby Jesus."

As we began worship one Sunday morning, I thought about how much the words of the song we were singing applied to Ken's life. God knew Ken before he was even a thought. He loved Ken with all his might and was doing a great work in him. I found myself wondering if God was able to speak to Ken through the worship songs, even if Ken wasn't able to understand what they meant in the same way the rest of us were. Notice that key phrase "in the same way the rest of us were." I was about to find out that he understood them on a level I wish everyone could.

Just as the chorus of the worship song was about to begin, I glanced over at Ken. Just as with every Sunday, there he was. He wore faded jean shorts and a striped polo shirt. His buzzed gray hair had a little cowlick in the back, and his stomach poked out a bit underneath his shirttails. His crystal blue eyes were sparkling with life. But something was different – very different. As the interlude of the song gave way to the chorus, Ken's eyes grew moist. Right along with rest of the congregation, as the chorus began he looked up and belted out "I am a flower quickly fading, here today and gone tomorrow; a wave tossed in the ocean, a vapor in the wind. Still you hear me when I'm calling. Lord, you catch me when I'm falling and you've told me who I am. I am yours."

I believe there's a time in every pastor's life where something happens that makes them realize that there's a point to everything they are doing, and God is truly using their ministry. Despite all the "emergencies" that come up at unexpected times, despite countless counseling sessions with church members about the same issue you thought you'd resolved the week before, something brings it all into perspective and makes it all worthwhile. At that point, Ken was that something for me.

While we were in charge of it, Safe Haven didn't have the funds to have their own building. We began as a house church, meeting each Sunday morning in our little two bedroom apartment. The apartment soon grew too small for our increasing numbers, especially with how many people in wheelchairs attended. We then moved to a covered picnic area in a nearby park. Each Sunday, Micah and I would drive to pick up a few members who were unable to provide their own transportation and would show up an hour or so early at the park to set up the communion table, test the sound system, and run through the order of worship with the participants.

For a small church, we sure got out in the community. We went regularly to a nearby nursing home with a "pet ministry," a bunch of us from the church who had various animals we brought to the people at the home to visit with and bring joy to their day. That was always a big hit. Micah's and my house was a zoo. We started out with two guinea pigs and nothing else and, by the time Safe Haven was going strong, we had six guinea pigs, with four more on the way, three hamsters and a hyperactive dog. Add to that two other dogs, a cat and two bunnies from other members and I felt like we had the Dr Doolittle mobile every time we left for a pet ministry trip.

We also went once or twice to the nearby Ronald McDonald house with the animals. The families, especially the siblings of the children who were in Children's Hospital nearby really enjoyed the laughs and love the animals provided. Pet ministry wasn't the only ministry of the church. We had taken a ministry idea from the church we had attended in San Bernardino and, each week, we put together grocery bags full of toiletries and non-perishable items to distribute to homeless people in the area.

Safe Haven became the little church that could. We weren't big, but we were strong, and we were very active in the community. We made the local newspapers a few times and had some of our members interviewed by reporters, but other than that things stayed relatively quiet. Micah and I had both begun working at this point on various pamphlets and articles pertaining to Christianity and the GLBT community. It was then that Micah and I started to formulate the idea of putting together a nonprofit organization that worked to help transsexuals with their transitions in a healthy and cost efficient way. Up to that point I had heard of way too many who were getting tainted hormones off the streets and cutting corners with illegal name changes and birth certificate forgeries. I'd done my homework and located several agencies in the area that would help my TS friends through their transitions. Our idea still hasn't taken off yet, but we hope it soon will.

Ministry was going great during that point in our lives. Unfortunately, that was about the only thing that was. Shortly before the founding of Safe Haven Community Church, I had been diagnosed with Bipolar 1 disorder, another medical whammy to face. The months following brought a barrage of different medications; anti-psychotics, anti-depressants, and mood stabilizers thrown in for good measure. I quickly came to realize that my body does not tolerate medications well. Other than Safe Haven, I remember very little about our time in Colton, as well as the last few weeks in San Bernardino. When we weren't doing church work, I slept. I didn't want to, but the drugs knocked me out so badly that even when I was conscious, I felt hazy. A majority of my life during that time was spent on the musty, tattered couches we'd salvaged from the curb a few months prior. To this day I'm amazed at the number of people who tell me what a positive influence I was in their life during that time. I can't even fathom how I could have been a help to anyone when I was in such turmoil myself.

Things were also very difficult financially. That, coupled with my illness, made for a horrendously stressful time. Safe Haven was plugging along masterfully, but its pastors were drowning in a sea of debt. We couldn't even guarantee food on the table from week to week. Assistance from Micah parents helped keep a roof over our heads, but we knew we could not continue living like we were. We began to pray that God would give us an answer as to what we were supposed to do.

Unfortunately, neither one of us liked that answer very much, myself much less even than Micah because of the fact that I was incapacitated enough at that point not to fully comprehend decisions until they had taken effect.. It wasn't very long before we both got a very clear sense from the Lord that our work at Safe Haven was done and it was time to move on. This made no sense, seeing as how we had just started working with Safe Haven a few months earlier and we didn't see how it would continue without being pastored.

Within a week, we received confirmation. Micah was speaking with a brother in Christ on the phone and he shared with Micah and with me that he felt like we were supposed to go back to where Micah grew up; North Carolina. At that point in my life, I wasn't in any position to argue with anything. I was over-medicated, over-tired and going through severe burnout. I agreed that, especially seeing as how the cost of living in North Carolina would be much cheaper and we had family out there to help us get settled, it might be a good idea. At the time that I agreed to this, I didn't even allow myself time to stop and think about everything we would have to leave behind. Until that point in my life, with that church and that group of friends I had never had anyone or anything in my life that I honestly thought I would have a horribly difficult time leaving behind. I would realize that later.

The decision was made in early October. We decided that we would move at the beginning of November. That way, there would only be one more time we'd have to worry about the exorbitant cost of rent at the apartment complex where we were staying. We decided it was time to tell the members of Safe Haven and the rest of our friends. I can honestly say the the news went over like a lead brick. It was clear that not only the church members, but also many of our friends felt abandoned and a bit cheated. It seemed to them and, honestly, even to us as though we had just started getting settled and doing a really good thing and then we were suddenly up and leaving. There was no explaining it.

As the time of the move got closer, things became more real to me and consequently much harder to deal with. I realized that I didn't know when or if I'd ever see many of my friends again. My friends in the area were just about the only friends I had, and I couldn't imagine having to start from scratch, knowing virtually nobody all over again. My depression hit rock bottom and I started to feel the bipolar taking more control of me than it ever had before.

The night before we were to leave for our cross country trek in our slightly less than comfortable Dodge Colt, I completely snapped. I stayed out half the night with a friend of mine after his birthday party, and didn't sleep at all that night. We got ready early the next morning and piled everything, complete with guinea pigs and dog in the car and took off. I didn't feel right. I suddenly started feeling like I needed to be back at the doctor's office. The stress was overriding the effects of the medication and I just knew something bad was going to happen. And it did.

Our car blew a flat tire in New Mexico. It was the straw that broke the camel's back. I couldn't do this. I couldn't leave California that fast, and move all the way across the country and leave everything and everyone I'd ever known. What happened next I still don't understand, but I somehow decided I wasn't going. I didn't know what that meant and, after the conversation that followed with my husband, he was pretty convinced I was divorcing him right then and there. In hindsight, I knew that what was happening was the lowest point of a nervous breakdown, but I didn't have the mental power at the time to verbalize it as such. The next thing I knew, Micah was dropping our animals off at a local pet store to be reclaimed, and I was boarding a greyhound bus, alone, back to Southern California. I didn't have a plan, didn't have money, or anything really more than the clothes on my back, and honestly didn't even have a reason. I hadn't even gotten on the bus before I realized I had made a mistake. I was too chicken, too humiliated to turn around and go back. In my mind, I had already irrevocably broken the heart of the only person I'd ever really loved so strongly. So I left.

I got back to Southern California about seventeen hours later. I spent the next week sitting on my friends' couch in Rialto, CA staring blankly at the wall feeling as though I was in a drugged stupor. I couldn't feel anything, couldn't see anything, couldn't hear anything. I was numb. It wasn't long until the unthinkable hell I was going through became more complex. One of my friends took me up to stay at his brother's house in Northern California. I went, amidst what I later found out were heated rumors of infidelity, sexual relationships with others than my husband, and countless other unthinkable accusations.

As I was so sick during the month that I stayed back in California, most of the time that I was there is now a very hazy dreamlike memory. I don't remember details. What I do remember is that everything I looked at, heard, saw and felt made me realize just how sick I really was. The fact that I couldn't feel anything scared me worse than anything. I couldn't feel hurt, anger, fear, pain, or even love.

Shortly after I moved to Northern California, I began talking with a counselor who helped me to see what was going on. She was someone who lived in that area, who I'd met on a web group a few months earlier. She knew I was bipolar. She also had a strong suspicion that the drugs I was on was making it worse rather than better. She instructed me to stop taking them at once, and to see how I felt.

I did. The first three days, I was dreadfully sick. After than, I started to come out of it. By the second week in December, I was coming around. I knew what I had to do, but didn't think I had the strength to do it. In the very throws of my illness, I had done the unthinkable and sent divorce papers and my wedding ring back to Micah. There was no way, in my mind, that he was going to take me back. Still, I had to try.

It was a Sunday. I should have thought about the fact that he'd probably be at church. My friend called him first. He didn't answer. I tried a few minutes later, and left a very shaky message on his answering machine. I waited. Half an hour, he called back.

You'd think, as a pastor, that I would know all about God's grace. That day, however, I learned just how far-reaching that grace was, and how it extends to each of us, no matter how badly we screw up. Micah and I talked for several hours that day, and several hours more every day for the next week. He actually understood, and he wasn't mad. He told me I sounded good, and that he could tell a change. I knew things weren't going to just go back to normal, but it sure seemed to be looking good that my marriage wasn't over.

On December 15, 2005 I boarded a plane home – to North Carolina. I have never been happier to see anyone in my life than I was to fall into my husband's arms that day. We stayed up and talked all that night. Things seemed good, really good. It didn't stay that good, though. I didn't stop to realize that, just as I had changed, so had he. There was a re-adjustment period that lasted for about the first month. We had more fights than I'd ever remembered having before, and I kept saying I wanted to leave, but thankfully I never did. I still wasn't completely well, but I was on the road to it.

The week that I arrived in North Carolina, Micah's family helped me to get involved with a mental health care provider in the area. They confirmed what I already had suspicions of - the previous doctors had me on very wrong medication for what I was dealing with. As it turned out, I was even allergic to one of the medications I was on. The doctors that evaluated me in North Carolina weren't even sure that at that point I qualified under the diagnosis of bipolar 1 disorder. They said I was clearly better than I had been before. Things were looking up. I shared with them about the anxiety I had been having even since being back and they decided to try me on two new medications that they thought I'd react better to.

Here we had another case of doctors practicing medicine. Within 24 hours, I was sicker than I had been in Colton. My sister in law, who is a nurse, said I had something called acathasia; essentially dizziness, lack of coordination, and sleepiness associated with a bad reaction to the medication I was taking. It took two weeks, but I convinced the doctors that the drugs were not right for me. I asked that they monitor me without medication for a while to see how I would do, and they finally agreed that would probably be best until they could get a better handle on what was going on.

Things got better instantaneously. I was having a tough time navigating the stairs in my brother-in-law's house where we were staying, so we decided to look for our own place. In the meantime, a friend of Micah's had agreed to let us stay at his place until the new apartment became available a few weeks later. During that time, our family also grew again. Micah knew how much I was missing the dog that we had left behind. We knew the chances of finding him ever again were almost nothing, so he agreed to take me to the local animal shelter to see what we could find.

I still remember that day. We walked to the back of the shelter where some of the smaller breeds were. One of the shelter workers was trying to lead us toward a small black and white border collie that she thought we would like. I barely looked at him. I knew with Micah's allergies a collie was completely out of the question. To be honest, I wasn't a fan of them anyway. However, a moment later I found something that I definitely liked. Just off to the right in one of the corner kennels was a small to medium sized dog – at least I thought it was a dog. It was soaking wet, covered in what looked like motor oil, and shivering with the cutest whimper I'd ever heard. I looked at her chart: "Terrier mix. Female. Three months old." I asked the shelter worker about her and found out she had been brought in a few hours earlier; found in a gutter covered in what indeed was motor oil.

We took her out of the kennel to get a closer look. Immediately, she started doing tricks, giving us hugs, and playing. We took her into the back to give her a bath and see what she actually looked like. "Rainbow," my husband and I said when she was clean. And that was what it became from that day. We brought her to our friend's house to stay with us until we could move into our new place, and she became part of the family.

On February 1, 2006 we were set to move into our new apartment in Morrisville, NC. Rent wasn't cheap, but it was better than it had been in California, and at least we were on our own. Unfortunately, we were also unemployed. Micah had landed a job at an insurance company not long after I got to North Carolina, which he didn't stay with long due to long hours and limited income. Luckily, just after moving to Morrisville I landed a job with an organization called the Arc of Orange County. I was to be a habilitation technician for children with developmental disabilities. I enjoyed it quite a bit. During that time, Micah got a job working graveyard shift at a similar organization. Life was nuts, with me working days and him working nights but at least we could pay the bills.

Things grew more complex when I left my job due to a serious pay cut, agreed to another job that was promised to me that summer, and was let go when I couldn't get to training because of floods in the area. Micah took a stop-gap job a few weeks later to try and help us out until we would be moving in August to our first home, a few hours away. Unfortunately the new job ended up being more short term than planned. After only a week, our car decided to call it quits. It was only two weeks until we would be moving, so at that point we both just gave up and started looking for employment out near where we'd be moving.

6

It is hard to imagine packing more than a quarter of a century into just one book, but here I've nearly done it. For now, as I sit in my living room in the first house we've ever owned, it is June 2007, and we have lived in our new home in Lumberton, NC for nearly a year now.

Life has changed for us significantly. I just passed the two year anniversary of being out of the closet as a bisexual. I've found, amazingly, that the people here in North Carolina, and even out in the seemingly barren country are far more supportive of my sexuality than those in California were. I am now completely out to everyone, and unashamed. I have lost friends, had members of my family spread rumors about my sex life that are untrue, and have even been banned from the college where I spent four years studying to be a minister. The trials, though, were not in vain. Though it was a long time coming, I can now say that for the last fourteen months I have held a BA in Religious Studies. While I did not complete my degree at Azusa Pacific University, I was able to find a college on the east coast that allowed me to clep out of several classes with proficiency tests and complete my degree with a 3.1 GPA.

Things are going well medically, too. Yes, I do and always will have Spina Bifida. However, after 21 years of having leg braces, things have improved to the point where I now get around with just forearm crutches. The sudden health improvements helped me to skirt a potential operation on my back it looked like I was going to have to have. That was really quite unusual actually. This past summer I had been scheduled for a spinal fusion because I have congestive lung disease as a result of my scoliosis. As they were doing the pre-op and scheduling the surgery date, the doctor called me and told me that something odd had happened. My x-ray had changed dramatically in just a few weeks time and the curvature had lessened to the point where I no longer needed surgery. Personally, I don't know what's so odd about that. God's not odd.

On the church front, things couldn't be better. I am knee deep in the middle of introducing the newly created Church of the Painted Sky mission to the surrounding communities. It's been much more slow-going than Safe Haven ever was. Four months after our first service, we still only have one regular attendee. However, we remain undaunted. All good things in God's plan take time. We've got experience now, and we know more about what a church needs to be success-ful. We are not a gay church, not a straight church, not a trans- gendered church. We are a Christian church, a community of believers working together to build up the Kingdom of Christ. And we are more than conquerers.

Our family continues to do well, and continues to grow. Micah and I are now pursuing the adoption process, after realizing just how many children here in North Carolina are in need of homes. It will be a long process, but well worth it. For now, we are content with our furry children; Rainbow, our year and a half old Tibetan Terrier, Oreos, our ten month old boston terrier/pointer hound mix, and Isaiah, our nearly six month old bull mastiff/carolina dog mix. They are the furry loves of our lives.

Actually, the past seven months we have gotten more than our fair share of dog experience. Back in December of 2006 my husband was coming home from work and narrowly avoided hitting a three week old lab puppy in the middle of the road. Since then, we have formed an official rescue, dubbed Laura's Ark, in honor of one of the founding members of Safe Haven and its pet ministry, who died late last year. Laura's Ark, to date, has rescued and re- homed nearly twenty five dogs. As I write this, our latest "middle of the road rescue dog" is bounding through our backyard chasing butterflies with her foster siblings. It's amazingly rewarding.

We still have our struggles. Finances are better than they've been in a while, but we're having to have more than a few mustard seeds of faith these days, as God has recently called us from secular work into full-time ministry. It's scary, and we often feel like we're venturing through life in the dark. However, as I gaze out the window at my husband engrossed in one of his many sci-fi novels in the back yard, and four lively balls of canine fluff hassling a pen full of chickens, I'm reminded of a line from one of my favorite country songs - "the view I love the most is my front porch looking in."

Afterword

When I set out to create Between Two Worlds, I had a mission. I described my mission at the beginning of this book. This book wasn't written just for bisexuals, or even just for Christians. It was for anyone who has ever been different; anyone who has ever stood out like a sore thumb in society. It was for all the misfits, the outcasts, the downtrodden, the social rejects. There is a place for you. My prayer for all who read this book is that if you know anybody who is hurting, anybody who is struggling, you find within yourself the courage to help them find the hope we all deserve.

In Galatians 3:28-29 we are told "there is neither Jew nor Greek, slave nor free, there is neither male nor female. We are one in Christ Jesus." Please, as you go about your daily lives, live this principle, whether you believe in Christ, or not There is so much more that unites us than what divides us. Life can be made right for those who suffer the pain of rejection by society. We all deserve love, life, and the respect we so desire.

978-0-595-45939-1
0-595-45939-0